FELTHAM

HANWORTH & BEDFONT

Gibbs' strawberry cart outside Bedfont church, 1900.

FELTHAM

HANWORTH & BEDFONT

A Pictorial History

Andrea Cameron

Andrea Cameron.
29th October 2002

Phillimore

2002

Published by
PHILLIMORE & CO. LTD.,
Shopwyke Manor Barn, Chichester, West Sussex

ISBN 1 86077 209 9

Printed and bound in Great Britain by
BIDDLES LTD.
Guildford, Surrey

List of Illustrations

Frontispiece: Gibbs' strawberry cart outside Bedfont church, 1900

Acknowledgements

The author would like to thank Hounslow Cultural and Community Services for agreeing to support this publication by allowing free access to the photographs in the Local Collection housed in Hounslow Library Centre. Mrs Brenda Matthews, Admin. Assistant, is thanked for undertaking the typing of the text and captions.

Most of the illustrations came from the Local Collection in Hounslow Library Centre but the following organisations and individuals are thanked for allowing photographs from their collections to be reproduced: Aerofilms Ltd., 61; Mr D. Biddle, 3, 9 , 20, 29, 35, 42, 136, 141, 147, 155; Mrs M. Brown, 6, 74, 96; Mrs A. Collins, 86; Mr D. Cotterell, 159; Mr J. L. Davies, 15, 16, 17, 18, 34, 64, 65, 66; Mr P. Downes, 30, 31, 55, 58, 90, 99, 105, 109, 111, 133, 149, 162, 185; English Heritage/NMR, 101, 168; Mr D. Gibbs, frontispiece, 135, 169, 170; London's Transport Museum, 78; Mr. D. Sherborn, 156, 163, 167.

A Brief History

Feltham, with Bedfont and Hanworth, forms the western part of the London Borough of Hounslow, established on 1 April 1965. From that date back to 1930, they comprised Feltham Urban District Council. All three villages have entries in the Domesday Survey of 1086 as manors within the Hundred of Spelthorne.

Feltham

There is no archaeological evidence of a Prehistoric or Roman settlement at Feltham. The first evidence is the entry in the Domesday Survey for the Manor of Felteha. Another early spelling is Feldham, meaning a village in a field. Felteha comes from Felte which was an English plant name.

Feltham was a very small, remote, agricultural village, completely surrounded by Hounslow Heath. The village centre was around St Dunstan's church and St Dunstan's Road. It was not until in 1848 the London and South Western railway line was constructed through Feltham that the centre moved to the High Street and the area around Feltham Green and pond.

Robert, Earl of Mortain owned the manor, which was only a nominal title, as jurisdiction over Feltham was invested in the neighbouring Manor of Kenyngton (Kempton). In 1228 both manors passed to King Henry III. Later King Henry VIII annexed Feltham to Hampton Court. After 1700 no manor courts were held and manorial rights died out. This did not affect lands owned by the Crown, which in 1631 were granted to Francis, Lord Cottington.

In 1634 a fire destroyed Lord Cottington's manor house, together with 13 dwelling houses and 16 barns, at a total value of approximately £5,000. Lord Cottington provided his 60 tenants with food and shelter, whilst their properties were rebuilt. Feltham Manor House was replaced and survived until demolition in 1966.

The first mention of a church in Feltham appears in a document of the 12th century, when the Countess of Lincoln gave the church to St Giles in the Fields. The first recorded Vicar was Petrus Whyt of Lincoln in 1322. Only one print survives of this church, which stood on the site of the present building. It was described as: 'a small structure, consisting of a chancel, nave and north aisle'.

The Longford River, which flows through Feltham, was constructed in 1638 on the instructions of King Charles I to provide work for idle soldiers. It comes off the

River Colne at Longford and winds its way across Hounslow Heath to Bushey Park, where it provides the Diana Fountain with a better water supply.

The oldest surviving house in Feltham is the Church Centre, next to St Dunstan's church. This 17th-century vicarage survived the 1634 fire. In 1976 a house in Cardinal Road became the new vicarage.

Today Feltham House is the most significant house, dating from the mid-18th century and possibly designed by James Wyatt. In the early 19th century it was a school run by Mr Augustus Frederick Westmacott, son of the sculptor, Sir Richard Westmacott. The sculptor's bust of the Rev. Edward Vale, Vicar of St Dunstan's church, may be seen in the church. The house became the Mess for the Royal Army Service Corps' Ordnance Depot during the First World War and is still retained by the army.

The oldest public house was the *Rose and Crown*. The original late 18th-century building survives as a private home in St Dunstan's Road. The *Rose and Crown* was rebuilt in 1940, when a new section of the High Street opened as a by-pass to St Dunstan's Road. At present this building is boarded up and unused. The oldest functioning public house is the *Red Lion* by Feltham Green, built *c.*1802. Threatened with demolition in 1969, it was granted listed building status and reprieved.

The second largest estate in Feltham was Hauburgers. This was situated on the north side of the High Street, between the Manor House and St Dunstan's church. By 1674 it was called Feltham Farm. In the 19th century it became a market garden run by Alfred Smith, who was known as the Cabbage King. The Grosvenor estate was built there in the early 1930s.

Almost opposite was Blaize Farm, with its 17th-century farmhouse. This was demolished in *c.*1932 for the Parkfield housing estate. At the junction of St Dunstan's Road with the High Street stood the 18th-century farmhouse Holly Farm. Demolished in *c.*1935, it is now the site of Holly Parade. In Spring Road there was Brook Farm, dating from the 18th century, but now occupied by 20th-century housing developments.

In 1800 James Lee and John Kennedy purchased four acres of ground described as 'Waste ground', backing onto the present Feltham Lodge. Lee and Kennedy were nursery men with extensive grounds in West London. Market gardening occupied the site until the 1930s, when it was sold for housing. Another famous nurseryman was Harry Veitch, who purchased land in *c.*1900 between Bedfont Lane and Road. In 1914 there was an auction of stock and the land was sold to Middlesex County Council for small holdings and allotments. In the late 20th century much of this land was built upon: two new housing developments and the Edward Pauling Primary School.

Sparrow Farm was established in the first half of the 19th century and survived until the 1950s, when the local authority developed the Sparrow Farm estate and built Sparrow Farm Primary School.

A vinery existed in the latter part of the 19th century. Owned by William Cole, it was called Grove Vineyard. Today it is commemorated by maisonettes called the Vineyards.

At the end of the 18th century St Dunstan's church was in need of restoration. In 1783 William Wynne Ryland was buried in the churchyard. Engraver to King George III, he was found guilty of forgery against the East India Company and executed at Tyburn. St Dunstan's church was demolished in 1801 and the present building consecrated in 1802. It consists of a nave, chancel and tower; a south aisle was added in 1855 and the north aisle in 1856.

The population in 1801 was 620; the village was still an agricultural community, but industry gradually arrived in the form of a flax mill. This was situated on the west bank of the River Crane, south of Baber Bridge. The spinning of flax ceased in 1835 and the mill was converted to snuff. By the end of the century it had become a cartridge factory.

A flour mill is recorded at Feltham Hill in 1800 and there were two blacksmiths by 1827. Mr Joseph Toussaint ran a wax chandlery business near Feltham Green. The Lodge family arrived in the late 18th century and developed businesses as bricklayers, builders and undertakers.

A number of houses were built at the end of 18th and beginning of the 19th centuries in the area of Feltham Hill. These included Cumbernauld Lodge, Groveley, Oak House and the Park. At the northern end of the village in 1802, Mr John Cole Steele had a house built on his lavender nursery ground. His lavender water shop was off the Strand. Every week he travelled from London on the stage coach to Hounslow and walked across Hounslow Heath to Feltham. One week he did not return to London and his battered body was found in a ditch by the Staines Road. It was 1807 before three men were arrested for his murder. One turned King's evidence and gained his freedom. Haggerty and Holloway were found guilty and executed outside Newgate prison. Such was the crush of crowds to view the executions that, when the street was cleared, 31 people were found dead and forty to fifty had been injured. His house was replaced in 1888 by Feltham Lodge, now home to Feltham Age Concern.

Feltham National School opened in 1839 and provided the first educational facilities for most children in the village. The school building was in the High Street, opposite the Green, where it functioned until 1876, when the Hanworth Road School opened.

In 1848 the London and South Western Railway extended their line from Richmond to Datchet, through Feltham. The population in 1851 was 1,109, an increase of only 80 since 1841, but by 1861 it had increased to 1,837. This shows that building developments throughout the 1850s followed the opening of the railway line.

The Middlesex Industrial Reformed School opened in 1859 on the borders of Bedfont and Ashford. Boys who were found begging on the London streets or committing petty crimes, and having no stable family background, were sent there to be educated. They left when they reached 12 years of age to take up apprenticeships or to go to Wales to work on sheep farms.

By the 1880s the population was over 3,000, with most people living in the area around Feltham station. In 1880 St Catherine's church opened, close to the station, as the chapel of ease for St Dunstan's church. Larger houses built in the 19th century were situated near St Catherine's church. These included Wilton Lodge and Bridge House. Public houses included the *Railway* inn, the *Crown and Sceptre* and the *Railway Tavern.*

Feltham High Street, from the station to Feltham Green, had shops along both sides by 1900. Cardinal Road School opened for boys in 1902. In the same year three businessmen financed the building of a Town Hall in Hanworth Road, before Feltham Urban District Council was established in 1903. The Council could not afford the Town Hall and in 1906 it became Feltham Magistrates Court.

New schools were built in the 1920s at Feltham Hill and Southville. These coped with the 1930s developments of new housing on land formerly farms and market gardens. These stopped in 1939 with the outbreak of the Second World War, but recommenced in the late 1940s, mostly with public housing. The opening in 1946 of Heathrow Airport provided employment for Feltham residents, and employees from other areas found homes in Feltham.

By the early 1960s plans for the creation of the Greater London Boroughs were underway, whilst Feltham U.D.C. was planning to redevelop the north side of the High Street and the land behind. Completion coincided with the establishment of the London Borough of Hounslow, providing the Feltham Centre shopping precinct and the Highfield Housing estate.

The south side of the High Street was developed in the 1970s with public housing and offices. In 1975 St Catherine's church, apart from the spire, was demolished and replaced by St Catherine's House, which incorporated the spire. Feltham Methodist Church was extended to become Christchurch, used by both Anglicans and non-conformists. More recent housing developments have been a mixture of private and housing associations. The Cineworld development in the late 1990s, on land once the offices of E.M.I., has provided welcome recreational facilities. At present Feltham is the recipient of Government regeneration money for rebuilding the Feltham Centre, and possibly a new library. The future for Feltham looks bright.

Hanworth

The name, comes from two Anglo-Saxon words 'haen' and 'worth' meaning a 'small homestead'. The Domesday Survey entry states that the manor was held by Robert under Roger de Montgomery, Earl of Arundel.

The first mention of a church occurs in a 1293 grant of the Manor. The first recorded Rector is Adam de Brome in 1315. He moved from Hanworth to be Rector of St Mary Magdalene, Oxford and founded Oriel College. His name was commemorated in De Brome School, now part of Feltham Community School. Oriel is the name of a primary school, opened in 1935.

St George's church was described as 'a small gothic structure of flint and stone consisting of a chancel and nave. At the west end is a low wooden turret.' This building was in use until the early 19th century.

By the late 15th century, Sir John Crosby, Alderman of the City of London, owned both Hanworth Manor and Crosby Hall, Bishopsgate. This medieval hall is now resited on the Chelsea Embankment. On Crosby's death the manor passed to the Grocers' Company, but on an exchange of lands it was transferred to King Henry VII, who used the house as a hunting lodge, whilst hunting on Hounslow Heath.

On Henry's death, his son, Henry VIII, who also loved hunting, became the owner. Prior to his marriage to Anne Boleyn, Henry spent money on the house, with new panelling, silk hangings and furniture. On his marriage he gave Anne the Manor for her lifetime. On her execution, Henry received the Manor back and after his death it passed to his last wife, Katherine Parr. She lived there with Henry's daughter, Princess Elizabeth. Katherine married Sir Thomas Seymour and, after Katherine's death, Thomas was accused of chasing the young Elizabeth in the gardens at Hanworth, catching her and tampering with her clothes. Elizabeth's nurse gave evidence to this effect and Thomas was found guilty of treason and beheaded.

Elizabeth I stayed several times at Hanworth Manor, hunting on Hounslow Heath. On a visit in 1600 she had one of her last portraits painted. The Killigrew family, courtiers to Elizabeth I, leased the manor until 1627, when it was transferred to Sir Francis Cottington, a courtier in the Courts of James and Charles I. Having been Ambassador to Spain 1629-1631, Cottington became Baron Cottington of Hanworth.

In 1635 Cottington entertained Queen Henrietta and her court to dinner. Throughout the Civil War Cottington supported Charles I and the Royalist cause. In 1642 Parliamentarian soldiers damaged his property at Hanworth. Cottington petitioned Parliament for the restitution of the arms stolen or money to replace them. This was dismissed because of his Royalist sympathies. A chest containing money and plate was returned to St George's church.

At the end of the war his Hanworth property was again searched for money. Cottington sought permission to go abroad with his goods and servants. This was refused so he left without permission and settled in Valladolid, where he died and was buried within an English College belonging to the Jesuits. At the Restoration, Cottington's nephew retrieved his estates. In 1670, his great-nephew, Charles, sold Hanworth Manor to Sir Thomas Chambers, whose family were sugar planters in Jamaica. Baron Cottington's body was exhumed in 1678 and returned to England, where it was buried next to his wife, Anne, in St Paul's chapel, Westminster Abbey.

Sir Thomas Chambers left the manor to his son, Thomas, who married Mary Berkeley of Cranford. It was their daughter, Mary, who inherited the Manor and married Lord Vere Beauclerk, third son of the 1st Duke of St Albans. After a career in the Royal Navy he was created Baron Vere of Hanworth. Their son, Aubrey, in 1786, became 5th Duke of St Albans and owner of Hanworth Manor.

In 1784 the army under General Sir William Roy was commissioned to make a measurement across Hounslow Heath from King's Arbour (now Heathrow Airport, North) to Hampton, passing through Hanworth Park. This became a base line triangulation from which the whole country was surveyed and the first Ordnance Survey maps were produced. This line still forms the basis of Ordnance Survey maps.

After the death of his wife in 1789, the 5th Duke of St Albans spent little time at Hanworth and the manor house was let to tenants. In March 1797 disaster struck, when a fire destroyed the house. Fire brigades from Sunbury, Hampton and Twickenham attended. Some accounts state that St George's church suffered fire damage, but the church records do not support this.

All that survived was the stable block and the coach house. In 1923 the stables were converted into flats, Tudor Court. More recently the coach house was converted into two homes.

A small house was built next to the manor ruins, but this was demolished in 1875 and replaced by Tudor House, now converted into flats. The 5th Duke of St Albans died in 1802 and was succeeded by his son, Aubrey. In 1811 he sold off a large part of the estate including Hanworth Park.

In 1808 the Vestry minutes of St George's church record that the church was to be demolished and a new one built, re-using existing stone. The architect was James Wyatt, who lived at Hanworth Farm, now the site of the South West Middlesex Crematorium. The church, consisting of a nave, with a vestry room at the east end, was consecrated in 1813. James Wyatt was killed in a coach accident travelling from Bath to London in 1812.

Hanworth Park House was built in the period 1820 to 1840 in Hanworth Park. In 1840 the house and 463 acres of the Park were sold to Henry Perkins, a partner in Barclay, Perkins and Company, brewers of Southwark. He died in 1855 and was buried in St George's churchyard. His son Algernon inherited the estate and was responsible for having the clock tower and wing added to Hanworth Park House.

In 1865 Algernon paid for the chancel and spire to be added to St George's church, designed by Samuel Teulon, architect of Sandringham House. Like Feltham and Bedfont, Hanworth did not have a school until Queen Victoria's reign. Hanworth National School in Park Road was built in 1847 on land given by Henry Perkins. The first headmaster was Mr James Mindenhall, who retired in 1874.

At the end of the 19th century William Whiteley, owner of Whiteley's store in Bayswater, purchased Butts and Glebe Farms, giving him 200 acres of farmland. Renamed Hanworth Farms and bounded by Hampton Road, West, the Hounslow Road, Staines Road, West and the River Crane, everything sold in the store's Food Hall was produced here. Animals were reared and slaughtered, crops were produced, and there were canneries and jam making factories. The products left Hanworth daily by horse and cart for Bayswater. This continued until in 1907 William Whiteley was murdered by his illegitimate son. His legitimate sons took over and sold Hanworth Farms to Mr T.W. Beach, a jam manufacturer, who continued operations at Hanworth until 1933. The site was then sold to New Ideal Homesteads, who developed the area with suburban housing.

The population of Hanworth increased during the 19th century from 334 inhabitants to 1,309 in 1891, and 1901 saw the population increased to 2,159 inhabitants. To cope with this Hanworth National School was extended in 1873, 1878 and 1894.

The Hanworth Farm Estate became known as Little Hanworth Park in the 19th century and was purchased by Sir Frederick Pollock in 1834, giving him estates at both Hatton and Hanworth. In 1866 he built Woodlawn and in 1867 the Oaks. These were lived in by his children and both houses survive.

In 1873 Hanworth Park was sold to Mr Alfred Lafone, M.P., who died in 1911. Hanworth Park House remained empty until 1915, when it became a British Red Cross army hospital for wounded soldiers. In 1916 the estate was sold to Mr James Whitehead, an aircraft manufacturer, who wished to use the Park as an airfield. For this to happen, part of the Longford River had to be culverted. Mr Whitehead already had an aircraft factory at Richmond, but now built a second one on the borders of Hanworth and Feltham, in Victoria Road. Some of these buildings survive.

Mr Whitehead went into voluntary liquidation in 1919 and the early 1920s were occupied by bankruptcy proceedings. A Garden Suburb development for 1,800 houses was proposed in 1923 but came to nothing. In 1928 it was announced that Hanworth Park was to become the London Air Park. Flying and aircraft development took place throughout the 1930s and the Second World War. Companies based there included National Flying Services, General Aircraft and Cierva Autogiros. Large airshows took place each summer, and the Graf Zeppelin airship landed in 1931 and 1932. Hanworth Park House became the clubhouse and hotel.

In 1946, with the opening of Heathrow Airport, flying ceased at Hanworth. *Hanworth Park Hotel* continued until 1953 when it was sold to Middlesex County Council and became a residential home for the elderly. Feltham UDC in 1949 commenced negotiations to purchase the Air Park as a public open space. In 1959 this opened as Hanworth Air Park.

The late 1960s saw planning of the M3 motorway from Sunbury to Southampton. The motorway feeder road would come through Hanworth along the lines of the Twickenham Road and Sunbury Way, cutting Hanworth in two. In preparation for this, Forge Lane Infants and Junior School was built on the Hampton side of the road. Hanworth Library was rebuilt at the Mount junction; the *Brown Bear* public house was demolished and the War Memorial re-sited.

The M3 feeder road was constructed in 1973. Housing developments on the borders of Hanworth and Hampton took place during the 1970s on nursery and market garden land. Today, however, Hanworth retains more open space than many areas within the borough.

Bedfont

The Domesday Book entry refers to Bedefunde. The derivation is given as 'Bed', a personal name, and 'funta' meaning spring. Literally, Bed's spring or well.

The parish, called East Bedfont with Hatton, stretches east to west along the Staines Road from Baber Bridge to the boundary with Ashford. The Staines Road is the Roman road 'Via Trinobantes' from London to Silchester.

There is no archaeological evidence of a Roman settlement, although at West Bedfont, to the north, there are signs of a causeway and an Iron-Age settlement.

Domesday Book states that Bedfont was owned by Richard under Walter son of
Othere. A separate manor of Pates or Paites was held by Robert, Earl of Mortain.
Pates Manor survives as a medieval hall house of the late 15th century with a
16th-century wing. Robert, Earl of Arundel, Walter de Mucedont and Walter son
of Othere held land in Hatton.

The village centre has always been around Bedfont Green, where the parish
church dedicated to St Mary the Virgin is situated. This is the oldest church within
the Borough of Hounslow, founded c.1150. The Norman chancel, chancel arch and
south doorway survive from the 12th century. Two recesses to the north of the
chancel arch contain medieval wall paintings of c.1240-50. These were uncovered
in 1865, when part of the church was re-built. The painting in the east recess
depicts the Crucifixion whilst that in the north recess shows Christ enthroned.

Bedfont was an agricultural community from the Norman period up to the 20th
century. The Enclosure Map of 1817 shows much of the parish divided into the strip
field system of Norman times. The Manor of East Bedfont was owned from c.1313 by
the Trinitarian Priory of Holy Trinity, Hounslow. After the Reformation it passed to
the Crown and from them to the Berkeley family of Cranford, who in 1656 sold it
to the Earl of Northumberland. The industries that grew up along both sides of the
Roman road serviced the continual stream of travellers to and from London and the
West Country. These were the inns, stables and blacksmith forges. Travellers from the
West Country brought wagons loaded with wool, grain and vegetables. Drovers from
Wales and the west brought cattle to Smithfield Market. Bedfont is unique in having
two surviving manor houses: Pates Manor, already mentioned, and, on the south side
of Bedfont Green, Fawns Manor. The house dates back to the mid-16th century with
17th-century additions. The Sherborn family are recorded in Bedfont from the 14th
century and owned Fawns Manor from the 17th century until the early 1980s, when
Derek Sherborn sold the house and grounds to the British Airways Housing Association. It is now divided into six flats.

In 1630 Hounslow Sword Mill was established at the eastern end of the parish
on the banks of the Duke of Northumberland's river. Licensed by King Charles I,
German swordsmiths were brought from Solingen to produce one thousand
swordblades per month. Today Hounslow swords are highly collectable and
Gunnersbury Park Museum is fortunate in owning a number. During the English
Civil War, one of the sword makers, Benjamin Stone, followed King Charles I to
Oxford. The Hounslow Mill was seized by Parliament and in 1654 was converted
to a gunpowder mill.

The Bedfont Gunpowder Mill used the sword mill, besides new mills built closer
to Baber Bridge, in an area now known as Donkey Woods. Gunpowder manufacture
was very dangerous and there were many explosions in which employees were killed
or maimed and the mill buildings were demolished and rebuilt. The land on which
the gunpowder mills stood was owned by the Earls and Dukes of Northumberland.
A number of different people ran the mills during the 18th century. Then in 1833
Messrs Curtis and Harvey took over the lease and in 1871 they purchased the

freehold from the Duke of Northumberland. In 1922 they were absorbed by Imperial Chemical Industries, who closed the mills in 1926.

During the 17th-century English Civil War both the Royalist Army and that of Parliament travelled through Bedfont. The Parliamentarian Army on several occasions camped on Hounslow Heath, which surrounded the village.

Widow Harman, who leased Pates Manor from Christ's Hospital, complained that she should have a reduction in her rent as she had both the King's and Parliament's troops billeted on her. Both sides caused damage to the house and her furniture.

By 1700 there were a number of inns along both sides of the road through Bedfont. One of the oldest was the *Talbot*, later known as the *Black Dog*. This was situated on the Staines Road, at the junction with the Hatton Road and looked out over Bedfont Green. Other early inns were the *Rose*, the *Roebuck*, the *George* and the *Red Lyon*. A survey of 1686 records Bedfont as having seven guest beds and stabling for 18 horses.

The road became known as the Great Western Road and its upkeep through Bedfont was a parish responsibility. Each year two Highway Surveyors were elected by the Vestry and each able-bodied man in the parish had to give three days' labour per year to repairing the roads. In 1727, 230 local gentry and farmers petitioned Parliament for an Act for Repairing the Road from the Powder Mills on Hounslow Heath to Basingstoke. This came into effect in 1728 with The Bedfont and Bagshot Turnpike Trust. Turnpike gates were erected along the road and tolls were charged to travel from turnpike to turnpike. The Bedfont turnpike and toll house were erected on the border of Bedfont with Ashford.

The first stage coach services between London and the West Country began in the 17th century as did the Royal Mail service, which allowed people to send letters by the King's postboys. Regular stage coach services between London and Cornwall developed throughout the 18th century. The mail coach, which took both mail and passengers and took precedence over a stage coach, commenced in 1784. The Silver Mail Coach, between London and Exeter, came through Bedfont.

More inns appeared throughout the 18th century. On Bedfont Green were the *Bell* and the *Duke's Head*. Others included the *White Horse*, the *Plough*, the *Sun* and the *Queen's Head*. Detached houses were built around Bedfont Green and along the Great Western Road. On Bedfont Green, St Mary's or Burlington House, built *c*.1790, survives next to Bedfont church. Along the Staines Road Bedfont House, now the David Henry Waring Home, and Bennett's Farm survive. In the Hatton Road St Mary's Vicarage was replaced by the present Vicarage in 1958.

The stage and mail coaches continued until the completion of the Great Western Railway from London to Bristol in 1841, when passengers changed to the railway and by 1847 both stage coach and mail services to the west had ceased. The Turnpike Trust and the tollgate continued until 1875.

During the 19th century many of the farms became market gardens, providing fresh vegetables and fruit for the London markets. The Enclosure Act for the Parish of East Bedfont, 1817, saw the end of the strip field system, as ownership was re-allocated to provide larger more economic fields.

In 1847 Bedfont National School in the Hatton Road was built on land given by Col. William Reed, of Burlington House. The one small building served as the Infants, Junior and Senior School until the mid-1930s when Longford School in Feltham opened near the boundary with Bedfont. The National School building continued as an Infants and Junior School until the present school opened in 1951.

The Victorian period·saw the building of smaller houses and rows of cottages along either side of the Staines Road. More public houses were built such as the *Beehive*, the *Load of Hay*, the *Duke of Wellington* and the *Royal Oak*. Bedfont Police Station was built adjacent to the *Load of Hay* in 1867.

The early 20th century saw little change but by the 1920s, motor traffic appeared on the main road and Gibbs, the blacksmith, who started business in 1844, became a motor garage. The firm continued to supply agricultural equipment and machinery until it closed in 1997. In 1925 the Great South West Road opened as an extension to the Great West Road. This allowed increasing motor traffic to by-pass the village centre. New suburban housing developments followed throughout the 1930s, on land which had for centuries been farms and market gardens.

A halt to this came with the Second World War, 1939-45, but continued apace from 1946. In this year, London Heathrow Airport opened, becoming the largest employer in the area, with ever increasing needs for housing. At the end of 2001, the result of the public enquiry gave permission for a fifth terminal. This will expand the airport westwards and have a major impact on life in Bedfont.

Hatton

In the north-east corner of the parish of East Bedfont lies the hamlet of Hatton. Today it is all but swallowed up by Heathrow Airport, but previously was a quiet agricultural community, completely surrounded by Hounslow Heath.

The *Green Man* public house is a building dating back in parts to the 17th century and recorded as having a licence since 1786. At Hatton is the 18th-century house called Blenheim. The largest house was the 18th-century Hatton House, remembered as Dick Turpin's Kitchen in the 1930s and 1940s. Nearby was Temple Hatton, the home of Sir Frederick Pollock from *c*.1834-70. At the end of the 19th century it became an orphanage called St Anthony's Home.

Also at Hatton was Steam Farm, whose farmhouse survived until the 1960s. Opposite, at the start of Hatton Road, an 18th-century barn survives, which in Victorian times became a chapel of ease for the parish of East Bedfont. This has recently been restored and converted to an office.

Today Hatton Cross underground station preserves the name of an all-but-lost hamlet.

Feltham

1 The lodge entrance to the Middlesex Industrial Reformed School, Bedfont Road, *c.*1910. Opened in 1859 as a boarding school for boys found guilty of petty crime, it was purchased in 1910 by the Prison Commissioners for conversion into a borstal. The Victorian buildings were rebuilt in the 1970s as Feltham Young Offenders Institute.

2 (*Above*) A view of the chapel and some of the Middlesex Industrial Reformed School buildings in 1920. During the First World War it was an internment camp for aliens, re-opening in 1919 as Feltham Borstal.

3 (*Left*) The tower with spire of the present St Dunstan's church, built in 1802, replacing a medieval building of the 14th century.

4 (*Right*) St Dunstan's church chancel as restored in 1923, showing a new altar made from oak which had been in the original church and a new marble floor. Right is the pulpit; all that survived of a triple-decker pulpit from the first church. In 1955 the oak panelling and choir stalls were removed and burnt, because of death-watch beetle and a virile fungus.

5 A head-and-shoulders marble bust of the Rev. Edward Vale, Vicar 1833-48, sculpted by Sir Richard Westmacott. This was first placed in Feltham National School, opened in 1839, but later moved to St Dunstan's church. The Rev. Vale was much loved but suffered ill health and died in office in 1848. He was buried in the churchyard.

6 The Rev. John Francis Jemmett, Vicar of St Dunstan's church, 1877-1911, photographed with the Rev. C.H. Wood, curate 1904-08.

7 A St Dunstan's church charabanc outing to Burnham Beeches in 1907. Seated in the driving seat from the left: B. Adams, K. Fryer, W. Lee Uff. The two gentlemen standing below are H. Lee Uff and T. Parker. As many of the passengers are girls it was most likely a Sunday School outing.

8 The original village centre in St Dunstan's Road, photographed *c.*1900. Left is the turning into Bedfont Road. The *White Lion* public house on the right closed in the 1930s and is now a car repair business. In the distance is the *Rose and Crown* public house, built *c.*1760 and closed in 1940. The building remains as a private home.

9 St Dunstan's Road, *c.*1910, when it was part of the main road from Feltham to Ashford. The *Rose and Crown*, right, opened *c.*1760 and closed in 1940, when the public house was rebuilt on a newly opened stretch of the High Street. On the left is M. A. Windiate, grocer.

10 Spring Cottages, *c*.1928, showing St Dunstan's church in the background. This is now the site of Spring Road. The cottages dated back to *c*.1800 and would have provided homes for agricultural labourers working in the market gardens. The cottages were demolished after the Second World War.

11 Brook Farm, Spring Road, *c*.1900. This thatched farmhouse dated back to the 18th century. On the right is the *Three Horseshoes* beerhouse and smithy. All these buildings were demolished in the mid-1930s and the present houses in Spring Road were built.

12 The *Three Horseshoes* beer house in the 1920s, showing a motor charabanc leaving with regular customers for a day's outing. The beer house was replaced in the late 1930s by the present public house on the High Street at the junction with Sunbury Road.

13 A procession of 1,400 school children, celebrating King Edward VII's coronation in August 1902. This had been postponed from June as the King was ill. On the Green an oak tree was planted by Mrs Fear. The children sang before following a band to Lower Feltham, where Mr A.W. Smith loaned a field. Here entertainments were provided and tea was taken in his barn.

14 Groveley House, Feltham Hill, photographed in the 1920s. The house was built *c*.1840 and in 1865 was called the Grove, but by 1890 was called Groveley. It was demolished in the 1950s, and Kinross Close and Drive were built on the site.

15 The garden of the Park, Feltham Hill, showing the side of the house built in *c.*1840, but much altered in *c.*1870. It was the home of Mr A.W. Smith, the market gardener, from *c.*1909 until his death in 1927, when it was sold. It was later known as Meadhurst and today is BP Amoco's Meadhurst Sports and Social Club.

16 The grounds of the Park in the 1920s, whilst the home of Mr A. W. Smith. Photographed on the occasion of a family celebration, possibly a wedding, it shows large limousines parked with their chauffeurs lining the railing by the flag pole.

17 Mr Alfred William Smith (1856-1927) as a debonair young man. Born in Roehampton, Alfred started market gardening off the Staines Road at Bedfont. After land was purchased in Feltham next to the *Sawyer's Arms* public house, Alfred lived at Burnham Villa, Feltham Hill. Eventually he owned 250 fruit-growing acres and many more for green vegetables, giving him the name of Cabbage King at Covent Garden market.

18 Three of Mr A.W. Smith's daughters photographed on the drive in front of the Park in the early years of the 20th century.

19 A foreman of the tomato house situated near the Sunbury border, possibly owned by Mr A.W. Smith, the largest market gardener in Feltham, *c.*1900. He leased 30 acres of land at Feltham Hill Road, stretching towards Sunbury. Here he had seven large greenhouses growing tomatoes. His glass house foreman was Mr Henry Bannister of Hounslow.

20 Geo. S. Watkins' wholesale ironmongers was situated on the High Street between the Manor House and Feltham Farm. They opened between 1890-99, when the owner was S.H. Watkins. By 1904 George was the owner, but by 1909 the premises were empty. In 1914 the owner was John Mahon, a farmer.

21 London House, 106 High Street, was situated at the junction of Manor Lane. This photograph of the First World War period shows the shop as a men's and ladies' outfitters called Toplis. They functioned from *c.*1910 until the mid-1930s. The building survived until the mid-1960s, but had been demolished by 1968.

22 Feltham High Street around 1910, looking towards Feltham Green. On the left is Feltham Independent church, built in 1865 and demolished in 1962 for road widening. It was replaced by Feltham Evangelical church in Manor Lane. The site beyond the lamp-post on the left is now Tesco's store, opened in 1993.

23 A narrow lane running from Feltham High Street towards Hanworth Park and parallel with Elmwood Avenue, *c.*1900. The gate on the left led into the garden of Feltham House. The lane disappeared after 1915 when the Royal Army Service Corps depot was established.

24 A March from Feltham Green on 17 April 1920 to protest about the footpath from the High Street into Hanworth Park, which was blocked off, under the Defence of the Realm Act, during the First World War, due to aircraft construction for the Royal Flying Corps. 2,000 people knocked down the wall. Filmed by the Gaumont Film Company, seen right, it was shown in cinema newsreels around London.

25 The level crossing in Feltham High Street, *c.*1959. This was a single track railway, off the Waterloo to Windsor line, and went down to the Royal Army Service Corps depot. This opened in 1915. The line was removed in the early 1960s, when the north side of the High Street was redeveloped. Right is the Lodge family's home, demolished at the same time.

26 Feltham pond on the Green, *c.*1900, with local boys posing for the photographer. The house on the right was Wilton Lodge, an early 19th-century building demolished in 1935 for the building of Wilton Parade. The building on its left was the *Cricketers* beer house.

27 Feltham fair took place on the Green from at least 1886 through to 1925 and was held at the beginning of May. In 1925 it is described as 'the annual assemblage of gipsies, bushers and vagabonds' and Feltham Ratepayers' Association were asking Feltham Council to stop letting the Green for the annual fair.

28 The christening of Feltham's first steam-driven fire engine on the Green in 1905. Purchased for £250, this was second-hand. Driven at first by horses and later by the Council's Tin Lizzie Ford lorry it served until the petrol-driven Morris commercial vehicle was purchased in 1933.

29 The inscribed panel on the Feltham Cenotaph recording the names of the men from Feltham killed in the First World War. The cenotaph situated on the edge of the Green was unveiled by Rear Admiral Sir Roger John Brownlow Keyes, R.N., Bt., in October 1920. Made of Portland stone, it cost £370, raised by public subscription.

OUR
ILLUSTRIOUS DEAD
1914 — 1918

ADAMS GEORGE	EDMEADS GEORGE	MANSFIELD HARRY	RYAN JOSEPH
BATES JOHN J.	ETOO ARTHUR	MANSELL ALBERT	SALTER WM
BAX JOHN W.	FLOCKHART FREDK H.	MAKSEY GEORGE A	SAMWORTH JOHN A.
BILLINGHURST D. C.	FREEMAN WALTER J.	MARSHALL ALBERT E.	SANGSTER FERGUS A.
BLACKWELL ERNEST	GARDENER HARRY	MATTHEWS WM	SCOONES F. V.
BRANDON ERNEST	GARDNER JOHN	MCMAHON FREDK E.S.	SCOTT ALFRED
BROWN CHAS E.	GARDNER WM	MEIKLE ORD S.	SCOTT ALFRED C.
BROWN FREDK C.	GLADING ARTHUR	MORRIS ARCHD C.	SELWOOD JOHN
BURGESS FREDK E.	GLADING FREDK C.	MORRIS C. DWIGHT	SIMMONDS WM H.
BUSHNELL JOHN W.	GODDARD CHAS	MUSK WM A.	SKITTRALL GEORGE
CADMAN PERCY	GREEN JOHN W.	NEALE WM	SMITH W. WYVILLE
CARTER JOHN	HALL ALBERT W.	NEAVE CECIL W.	STROUDWICK HARRY
CHALLIS CHAS J.	HALL HARRY A J.	PAGET ALBERT H.	TEDDER ERNEST
CHERRY ROBT E.	HATCH SIDNEY	PEATS EDWARD J.	TEDDER MATTHEW
CHILTON JOHN	HATCHER JOHN	PHILLIPS JOHN G.	TEDDER GEORGE H.
CLARK FRED	HAWKINS JOHN R.	PRIPPS JOHN	TILLYER HERBT C.
COLEMAN FREDK	HEMPSTEAD CHAS	PRICKETT WM G.	TILLYER HENRY P.
COLLIER FREDK	HOLDING WM C.	PRINCE ALFRED W.	TILLYER REUBEN A.
COLLINS CHAS	HOSKINS HERBERT	RADFORD BERNARD	TOCOCK CHAS L.
COOK CYRIL F.	HURWORTH ALFRED C.	RADFORD JOHN	TRIPP FRANCIS G.
CORRY ROWLAND	ISAACSON WM W.	RAY ALFRED J.	TURNER CHAS F.
COX CHAS	JEWELL FREDK	RAY FREDK J.	WEBB CHAS
COX HARRY	JOHNSON CHAS E.	REDDEN JAS	WEBB JOSEPH
CROMWELL GEORGE W.	KEVAN FREDK J.	REDFORD ARTHUR	WEEKS GEORGE J.
CROOK HARRY	KITNEY BERT	REDFORD GEORGE	WELLS GEORGE
CROXFORD WM C.	LANE FRANK	ROBERTS J. WM H.	WHEELER GEORGE F.
CURL THOS H.	LANE-NALL ROBT	ROBERTS WM	WHITE PERCY
DAY ARTHUR	LEWIS ERNEST J.	ROBINSON HAROLD	WINCH EDMOND A.
DARE CHAS	LITTLEWOOD THOS	ROBSON ROBT C. B.	WOODS WM
DICKENS WM	LOVICK GEORGE	RUSSELL LEONARD C.	WORSFOLD HENRY
DUNBAR ALFRED	LYNCH HENRY	RUSSELL SYDNEY	MERRICK CHAS
GARDNER WM	HASLER SAMUEL	SCOTT CECIL J.	SUTER FREDK C.
GILPIN JOHN L.	HOSKINS ALBERT	SKINNER ALBERT E.	ROBBINS HARRY

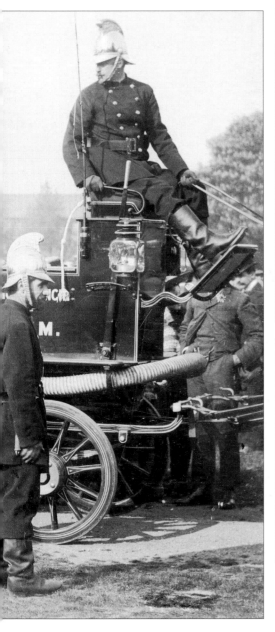

30 The re-built St Lawrence's Roman Catholic church, after the original building of 1912 was destroyed by fire in 1915. This church was in use until the present church opened in 1932. The building then became the parish hall and is still used as such.

31 The present St Lawrence's Roman Catholic church and adjacent Presbytery, built in 1932. The parish hall, previously the church, is reached via the gateway to the right of the presbytery. Mass was first said in Feltham in Mr Allan's house, Crendon Lodge, from the early years of the 20th century.

32 A view from Browells Lane into the garden of Feltham House, *c*.1900. A grazing horse can be seen in the centre right of the photograph.

33 The entrance gates to Feltham House from Browells Lane, *c*.1920. A section of the house can be glimpsed between the trees.

34 Feltham House, *c*.1900, whilst the home of Mr A. W. Smith. Built in the mid-18th century, the two side wings were added in the late 18th century. From *c*.1840-50 it was a boys' boarding school run by Mr Augustus Frederick Westmacott. In 1915 the house and surrounding land was taken over by the Royal Army Service Corps and the house became the Officers' Mess.

35 Knights and Newlyn were a ladies' and gentlemen's outfitters at 66-68 High Street, next door to the original *Cricketers*. They opened 1905-8 and were in business until *c*.1935. By 1939 they had been taken over by George Arthur Greenfield, who in turn had gone by 1960. The building was demolished in the early 1960s for re-development.

36 Feltham High Street, *c.*1958, showing right, the edge of Wilton Parade. The building with the shutters opened *c.*1862 as a beer house called the *Cricketers*, run by the Taylor family. It became a licensed public house *c.*1934, in new premises at 40 High Street.

37 Feltham High Street, *c.*1920, looking towards the railway bridge from the Post Office, seen extreme right, and Greenfield Bros. draper's shop on the extreme left.

38 Feltham High Street, *c.*1912, looking towards the railway bridge with Barclays Bank on the right, with, next door, Caxton Press run by Mr Hedges. Next came a grocer's shop run by Mr L. Christian, with a second grocer's shop run by Mr W.J. Moore. On the corner of Victoria Road was W.J. Robinson, saddler.

39 The *Cricketers* public house, built *c*.1934 at 40 High Street. This building was demolished in 1965 and replaced by a new public house in the Centre, which has now changed its name to *Moon on the Square*.

40 Feltham High Street in the 1950s showing two long-standing grocers' shops. Platt's Stores at 32 High Street was there by 1904 and did not close until 1964. Platt's Stores had shops throughout South West Middlesex. Pearks' Stores were in Feltham by 1914 at 16 High Street, but in 1930 they moved to number 26, where they remained until they closed in the early 1960s.

41 Jesse Handscombe's tobacconist, confectionery and seedman's shop was in Feltham High Street from the 1890s to *c*.1910, situated close to the Bedfont Lane turning. Their home was on the Staines Road at Bedfont, from where they functioned as a florist's and nursery garden until *c*.1939.

42 (*Above*) Feltham High Street *c*.1920, showing, right, a sign for a cinema. This was in New Chapel Road, the turning by the sign. The cinema opened in 1911, being converted from a Wesleyan chapel. It was called the Palace Picture Theatre, but in the 1920s changed to the New Cinema and *c*.1935 to the Roxy. It closed *c*.1938.

43   Cain's Farm Dairy was situated on the corner of a passage way leading to the Palace, Feltham's first cinema. The dairy was established in 1875 by Mr C. Glenie of Cain's Farm, situated off Cain's Lane in the parish of Harmondsworth, now part of Heathrow Airport. Mr Glenie died in 1906 and the dairy shop was taken over by Mr M. Hill.

44   Cain's Farm dairy cart, photographed at Cain's Farm in Harmondsworth. This was used to deliver the churns of milk to the dairy shop in Feltham High Street.

45 Looking down onto Feltham High Street from the spire of St Catherine's church, *c*.1904. Bottom left is the *Railway Hotel* with a horse and carriage outside. Bottom right is the turning into Bedfont Lane. Feltham High Street remained as narrow as this until redevelopment in the 1960s.

46 The *Railway Hotel*, built *c*.1850, shown in the early 20th century, whilst being run by the Harris family. John Harris was the landlord by 1862 until *c*.1880. Henry Pearcy Harris succeeded him and was landlord until *c*.1922. The hotel closed in 1935 and was replaced by the *Feltham Hotel*.

47 The newly-built *Feltham Hotel* in 1938. This is now the Feltham Community Association's Centre. Its last name as a restaurant was the Feltham Feast, which closed in the mid-1980s.

48 The Coronation Carnival procession of 6 June 1953 entering Feltham High Street, showing the Carnival Queen's float. The Carnival Queen was Connie Abbott. The procession formed in Burns Avenue and travelled along the High Street to Spring Corner. This was Feltham's first Carnival after the Second World War, and became an annual event.

49 J. Hyde opened as a baker in this shop on the corner of the High Street and Bedfont Lane between 1906-9. It had closed by 1928, when the premises were owned by Staines and Egham Co-operative Society Limited.

50 The Bedfont Lane turning, seen right, *c*.1958. The Co-op shop was given its façade in *c*.1935. It closed in the early 1960s for the Feltham Centre re-development. Tesco's supermarket opened there 1965. Extreme right is the *Prince of Wales* public house, which opened as a beer house in the late 19th century, and became a public house in the early 20th century. It was demolished in *c*.1981, for a McDonald's fast-food restaurant.

51 The *Queen's Arms* beerhouse, 29-31 Bedfont Lane photographed, *c*.1910. Standing in the doorway is Mrs Spary, wife of landlord Herbie Spary, with her children Herbert and Hettie. The beer house had closed by 1930 and became a greengrocer's shop. This closed in the 1970s and the site is now a car park.

52 The Queen's Arms building in Bedfont Lane during the 1950s. This shows it as a greengrocer's shop, owned by H. V. Mays.

53 The Mission Hall, Tachbrook Road, was established by the Primitive Methodists in 1884. The present Methodist church, Bedfont Lane, opened in 1928 and adjoined the Mission Hall, which became the Sunday School.

54 Three workers, *c.*1905, in William J. Songi's nursery garden beside 35 Fruen Road, where Mr Songi lived. The garden went through to Tachbrook Road and contained two large greenhouses. The nursery garden functioned through to the late 1940s, but had gone by 1960. Mr William Songi appears in local directories as a florist and greengrocer.

55 Feltham station house was built in 1847 ready for the opening of the London and South Western railway line from Richmond through to Datchet in January 1848. Feltham's station master would have lived on the first floor, when this photograph was taken, *c.*1900.

56 Feltham's only fire engine, *c.*1904, which consisted of one pump mounted on a horse and cart. The pump was worked see-saw fashion by a team of two men. This photograph was taken in the station yard, with the Station House in the background.

57 A carter or carman with his horse and cart outside the premises of Barber, Bellamy and Lorange, auctioneers, estate agents and valuers, *c*.1900. Their premises were in the Station Approach, but by 1914 had been taken over by Harris, Dundley Wand Co.

58 Feltham station in the 1920s looking towards Ashford. In the distance is the wooden footbridge in Bedfont Lane, built in 1912 and replaced by the present concrete bridge in 1928. The footbridge connecting the two platforms was constructed in 1888.

59 The personal inspection saloon of Mr D. Drummond, Chief Mechanical Engineer of the London and South Western Railway Company, 1895–1912. Seen on the footplate is Mr W. Eaton, shedmaster at the Feltham Motive Power Depot, photographed in the depot. Mr Eaton worked in the depot into the 1940s.

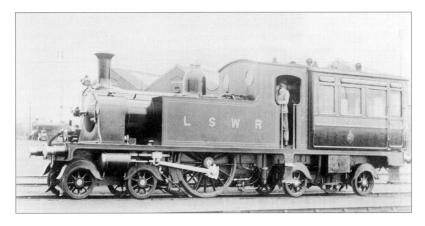

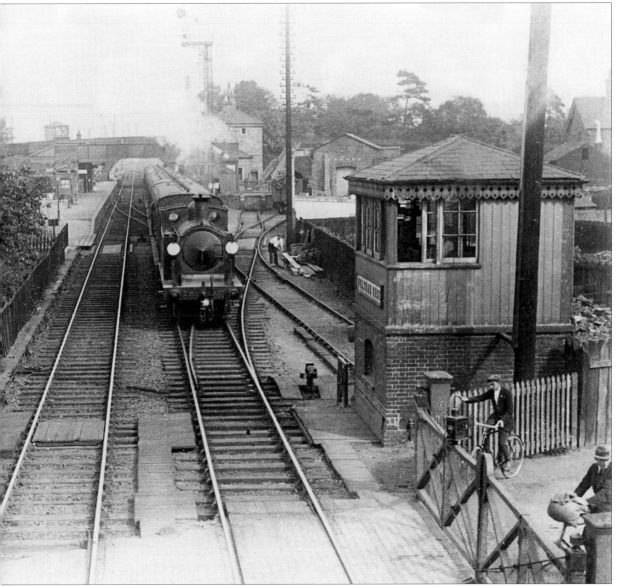

60 A steam train leaving Feltham station, *c.*1928. The London and South Western Railway line from Waterloo to Windsor opened in 1848. In the foreground is the level crossing, gated in 1876. The line was electrified in 1930 and the continental electronically controlled barriers were erected in 1974.

61 An aerial view of the Hounslow Road, *c*.1950, showing J.A. Parker's saw mills on the left with part of Feltham marshalling yard at the rear. Feltham station is seen top right. Land owned by the Parker family is etched with a black line around its perimeter.

62 Mr James Ashmead Parker, founder of Feltham Sawmills, photographed with his son Thomas, *c*.1930. The sawmills opened in *c*.1870 on the site of the present *St Giles Hotel*. As the sawmill prospered he purchased much of the surrounding land. A field in Hounslow Road given by him became a children's playground, called Feltham Recreation Ground. James Ashmead died in *c*.1932 and Tom in *c*.1952.

63 A terrace of four single-storey agricultural labourers' cottages on the Hounslow Road, behind the *Crown & Sceptre* public house. They were there by 1865 and are shown on the 1934 Ordnance Survey map, but had gone by 1963. The site is now occupied by terrace housing of the late 1930s.

64 Manor Farm, Harlington Road, West, opposite Feltham Lodge, existed by 1865 and was farmed by Edwin Barnham by *c.*1874. His son, Louis, succeeded *c.*1904, but sold to the builder and developer W.J. Drinkwater, who built the houses along that side of Harlington Road, West. Manor Farm was standing in 1934 but was replaced by the present houses in the late 1930s.

65 L/Cpl Louis Barnham, 3rd Middlesex Artillery, fought in the Boer War. He returned on 6 November 1900 and was seen by Irene Constance Smith, eldest daughter of Mr A.W. Smith, who determined to marry him. Louis and Constance married in 1904, living first at Manor Farm and then Feltham House and the Park, both homes of Mr A.W. Smith.

66 Irene Constance Smith, eldest daughter of Mr A.W. Smith, was born in 1882, possibly in Isleworth. This photograph of her in 1918 shows her as Mrs Louis Barnham and dressed as a nurse. This implies that she had been nursing locally during the First World War. She died in 1946.

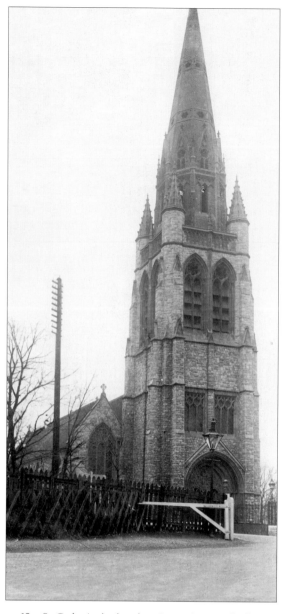

67 A 1938 advertisement for new houses being built in Buckingham Avenue by W. J. Drinkwater and Sons. The 1930s saw a number of building developments on market garden land. This stopped in 1939 with the start of the Second World War. After the War most of the housing developments were for Feltham U.D.C.

68 St Catherine's church, minus spire, was built in 1880 as the chapel of ease for the parish. The spire, added in 1897 in memory of Daniel Blake, buried in St Dunstan's churchyard in 1796, survives. The church was demolished in 1974 in preparation for a new church, which never happened, and Christchurch in Hanworth Road was created out of the Methodist church in 1981. In 1982 the site became an office development incorporating the spire.

69 St Catherine's church chancel showing, right, the brass eagle lectern presented in 1901 by Miss Shore in memory of her family. The pulpit was added in 1902 in memory of Frederick Lowton Spinks, who paid for the spire to be added in 1897-8. The east window was added in 1919 by the vicar, the Rev. Frederick. J. Browell in memory of his parents, who lived in the Grange, Browells Lane.

70 Hanworth Road looking towards the High Street junction in the early 20th century. On the left is part of the Hanworth Road School, built 1876. First used by infants, junior and senior children, it later became a primary school until 1974, when Victoria Road School opened. In the 1980s it housed Feltham Community Association and is now Cardinal Road Infant and Nursery School.

71 Bridge House, to the side of the railway bridge by Feltham station, took its name from the bridge. In 1931 the house became the offices of Feltham Urban District Council until the Civic Centre opened in 1976. Damaged by fire in July 1976, the house was demolished. A Social Security office, built on the site in 1980, was called Bridge House.

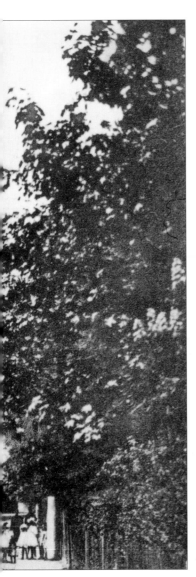

72 Hanworth Road looking towards the junction with the High Street in the early years of the 20th century. The distant turning on the left is Cardinal Road. The building with the small spire was built between 1865 and 1895 and was owned by the London and South Western Railway Company. Minus its spire it survives today.

73 The Magistrates' Court, Hanworth Road, was built in 1902 as a Town Hall. The words TOWN HALL show on the pediment above the entrance. Built as a speculative development by three businessmen, it was never used as a Town Hall. In 1905 the building was sold and converted into Feltham Magistrates' Court, which opened on the 2 April 1906.

74 Hanworth Road looking towards the Magistrates' Court, seen right. The photograph was taken during the First World War as women are shown sweeping the road. On the left, the spire is part of the Methodist church, opened in 1909. In 1981 this church was altered to become Christchurch, an ecumenical church used by Anglicans, Methodists and the United Reformed church.

HANWORTH PARK

75 Children playing in Hanworth Park, *c*.1910. The wooden bridge took the path across the Longford River. The path went from the Lodge gate in the Uxbridge Road across the park to Castle Way. The Longford River was culvetted under the park once it became the London Air Park.

76 Mr James A. Whitehead was a naturalised American citizen who set up an aircraft company in Richmond and purchased Hanworth Park in 1916 in order to use it for testing his aircraft. In 1919 White-head Aircraft (1917) Limited went into voluntary liquidation and bankruptcy proceedings started in 1920. In 1967 his daughter was still living in Richmond.

77 A First World War fuselage of a Sopwith Pup being taken from James Whitehead's factory at Richmond to Hanworth for assembling and testing in Hanworth Park, *c.*1917.

78 In 1925 the Union Construction Company acquired part of James Whitehead's aircraft factory in Victoria Road. Here they constructed carriages for the Central, Piccadilly and Bakerloo underground lines, plus a new metal frame tram, the Feltham. This Feltham frame is being towed by a Pickford steam traction engine to Fulwell depot for fitting out. In 1932 the Feltham site closed and moved to Fulwell.

79 General Aircraft Limited purchased William Whitehead's buildings at Feltham in 1934 and built planes there until 1949, when it merged with Blackburn Aircraft to form Blackburn and General Aircraft Limited and moved to Brough, Yorkshire. This photograph shows some of the 89 Hawker Fury II fighters built at Hanworth for the RAF in 1936-7.

80 Hanworth Park House in 1915 became a British Red Cross hospital. Sister Zala, a hospital matron from British Columbia, volunteered for overseas nursing. Here she is photographed on the steps of the house with some of her patients. Back row from the left: two unnamed Australian soldiers; Pte. Stewart, Australia; Pte. C.E. Nash, Australia. Front row from the left: Cpl. J. Willis, New Zealand; Pte. Laurence, New Zealand; Sister Zala; Pte. Carl H. Goodman, Canada.

81 *Hanworth Park House*, c.1935, was a hotel and clubhouse for the London Air Park. Built c.1820 for the Duke of St Albans, the side wing and clock tower were added for Algernon Perkins, c.1860. The hotel closed in 1953 and the building became an old people's home. This closed in 1992 and there are plans to turn it into a hotel.

82 The entrance hall of *Hanworth Park House*, *c*.1953, showing it as it was when it became a hotel in the 1930s.

83 The Graf Zeppelin airship visiting the London Air Park in August 1931 or 1932. The airship landed at Hanworth in both years. Over 40,000 people came to watch and 200 Middlesex Rover Scouts held the ropes to keep it on the ground.

84 London Air Park in the 1930s, showing a selection of bi-planes on the ground. The Air Park was forced to close in 1946, when Heathrow Airport opened. Feltham Council purchased the Park in 1956 for £110,557 and it opened as Hanworth Air Park, a public open space in 1959.

HANWORTH

85 Rookery Cottages, Elmwood Avenue, are the last buildings in Hanworth. Immediately to their right is the boundary between Hanworth and Feltham parishes. Photographed in *c*.1920, the cottages were built in *c*.1894, when Mr William Whiteley purchased the Rookeries estate. This comprised the Rookeries house and 34 acres of land. Here vegetables were grown for Whiteley's store.

86 The lych gate to St George's church, with the Hanworth policeman, Mr Fickling, photographed with his bicycle *c*.1919. His granddaughter, Mrs Collins, lives in Hanworth. The lych gate was built in 1882 to the memory of L.E.C., mother-in-law of the then Rector, the Rev. John L. Winslow.

87 This photograph of St George's church, *c*.1900, shows the second church, built in 1812-13 to a design by James Wyatt. The chancel and spire were added in 1865, designed by Samuel S. Teulon, architect of Sandringham House, Norfolk. The original church was an early 14th-century building.

88 The chancel of St George's church, *c*.1925, showing the new oak rood screen erected under the chancel arch, 1914, in memory of Alfred and Jane Lafone, of Hanworth Park House. This has since been removed and now forms the entrance to the north transept.

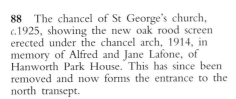

89 Castle Way from Hanworth Park, showing the path which leads across to the old Rectory. Behind the entrance gates can be seen Tudor House, built in 1875 for Mr James Scarlett who lived there until his death in 1903. The house is now converted into six flats.

90 Tudor House in 1917, used by the army to provide accommodation for troops. In 1923 it was sold to Mr James Hewat Mackenzie who converted the house into six flats for private occupation.

91 Tudor Court, *c.*1923, showing the 18th-century stables to Hanworth Manor being converted into living accommodation. In 1923 Tudor House and the remains of the Manor house were purchased by Mr James Hewat Mackenzie, who financed the conversion. He and his wife lived in the cottage in Castle Way by the entrance into Tudor Court.

92 The inner courtyard of Tudor Court, 1959, showing the backs of two 18th-century statues, possibly purchased by the Duke of St Albans. The coach house on the right was converted into two dwellings during the 1980s.

93 Two Tudor fireplaces from Hanworth Manor survive in the grounds of Tudor Court. The right-hand one disappears into the flat of 6 Tudor Court and can be seen in the bathroom.

94 Queen Elizabeth's walk in the grounds of Tudor Court, *c.*1920, before the stable block was converted into flats. The side of Tudor House is seen in the distance.

95 A tree-lined walk in the gardens of Tudor Court in the 1920s, possibly situated along one side of the Moat. This site is now part of the Moatside housing development built in the early 1950s.

96   A soldier pushing his bike along Castle Way, *c.*1915, with Hanworth Park on the right. Either side of the white gate are two ponds. The gate is at the end of a path that led to St George's Rectory. The wall on the left is part of Tudor Court.

97   Sunbury Way from the turning into Feltham Hill Road, seen left, *c.*1930. This photograph shows the newly built houses in Sunbury Way. Today the M3 feeder road is sited to the right of the photograph.

98 Low Farm, Kempton Lane in the early years of the 20th century, when it was farmed by Mr A.W. Smith. Built in the late 19th century, the farmhouse was demolished, *c.*1966, for the building of Lindon-Bennett school, opened in 1968. Low Farm existed before the building of this house and had previously been the site of the original *Brown Bear* public house.

99 Main Street, *c.*1912, looking towards Swan Road, *c.*1910, showing Godding's Cottages on the left, built *c.*1912. On the right at the far end of the row of buildings was the *Half Moon* beer house.

100 The *Half Moon* public house, in Main Street, *c.*1930. Built in 1861 as a beer house, it was demolished in the late 1960s and replaced by the *New Moon* public house.

101 The front entrance to Hanworth House in Main Street, photographed in 1949, before its demolition in 1960. Built in *c.*1700, it was extended in the 18th and 19th centuries. Today only the coach house survives and the houses in St Alban's Avenue stand on the site of the house.

102 Edward and Louisa Cherry in their coalyard in Main Street, *c*.1907. They lived next door at 12 Frederick Cottages which survived into the 1960s, but by 1969 had been replaced by the present flats, numbers 89-99 Main Street.

103 The *Swan* public house, *c*.1905. This building dated back to at least 1800. It stood at the junction of Swan Road and Green Lane facing onto the Swan pond. In the 1920s the *Swan* was rebuilt and now faces onto Swan Road. The pond has been drained and the grassed area is now the site of the Hanworth War Memorial.

104 View of Swan pond, *c.*1900, showing cows making their way into the farmyard that was attached to the *Swan* pub.

105 Bear Road looking towards the Twickenham Road, *c.*1910. On the left is F. Crate, baker's shop, *c.*1890–*c.*1935. In the distance the horse and cart is in the Twickenham Road and beyond on the right is the house lived in by the schoolmaster. This was built in 1884 as the reading rooms. In the far distance is Hanworth National School.

106 The *Brown Bear* public house, *c.*1900, was the oldest pub in Hanworth. The original building had a licence by 1738 and stood in Nallhead Road, where the Lindon-Bennett School is now sited. It was rebuilt in the early 19th century at the junction of Bear Road with Sunbury Way and was demolished in 1973 for the M3 feeder road.

107 The unveiling of the War Memorial in November 1920, at the junction of Bear Road with the Twickenham Road and Sunbury Way. The Rector, the Rev. Fairfax Scott, has, on his right, Mr Ainslie, son-in-law of Mr Alfred Lafone, former owner of Hanworth Park House. The War Memorial had to be re-sited in 1973 for the building of the M3 feeder road.

108 The *Oxford Arms* public house, *c*.1910, showing an early three-wheeled motor car on the Twickenham Road. This building of 1896 replaced an earlier beer house on the site, at the junction with the Hounslow Road. Demolished in 2000, it was replaced by a block of flats on this site.

109 The Twickenham Road, *c*.1918, looking towards the *Oxford Arms*. The turning on the left is St George's Road, with Ridge's stores, a grocer's shop and post office on the corner. On this side of the cycle works is Geo. G. Slater's, confectionery shop, and on the extreme left is Geo. Sparks' newsagent's shop. All these buildings were demolished for the M3 feeder road.

110   The Splash, Twickenham Road, *c.*1910, showing a horse and cart in the Splash travelling towards the *Brown Bear* public house. The Splash was part of the Longford River, man-made in the 17th century. By 1934 a new bridge had been built across the entire span of the river.

111   An early 20th-century photograph of Hanworth National School in Park Road, originally built in 1848 on land given by Henry Perkins of Hanworth Park House. The school was extended in 1873, 1878, 1894 and 1907, by which time it could accommodate 565 children. In 1969 it was demolished. Forge Lane Primary School replaced it. The Hollands housing development now occupies the site.

112 Children from the Infants department of Hanworth National Schools, photographed with their two teachers in 1880.

113 The staff of Hanworth National Schools, photographed *c.*1895. Standing from the left: Miss Freebody, Gertrude Weston, Edith Marsh (later Mrs Everard). Seated on chairs from the left: Nettie Gulliford, Mr Kirby (Headmaster), Mrs Stannard (Headmistress), Miss Murray (later Mrs Gibbs). Seated on ground from the left: Nellie Matthews, Lottie Dennis, Rose Weston.

114 St George's Rectory, Hanworth Park was built *c.*1812, replacing an earlier building. In 1974 the present Rectory in Blakewood Close was built and the 19th-century building was sold to the Shaftesbury Homes. In 1985 it became a private boys' school, Hounslow College, which moved from Lampton Road, Hounslow. This closed in 2000 and it is now a school called Little Eden and Eden High Seventh Day Adventist School.

115 & **116**   The Rev. John and Mrs Winslow, *c.*1890. The Rev. Winslow was Rector of St George's church, 1879-1902, where both were much loved. Their son, the Rev. Jack Winslow, retained his links with the church until his death in 1974. He visited Hanworth each year to preach a sermon. In 1954 he wrote *Eyelids of the Dawn*, describing his parents' work in Hanworth.

117 Miss Violet Winslow, daughter of the Rector, John Lyndhurst Winslow, who lived in Hanworth Rectory 1879-1902.

118 Miss Emily Hubble, parlour maid at Hanworth Rectory, *c*.1890.

119 The Hounslow Road early in the 20th century, seen from the junction at the Mount. On the right is the narrow bridge, with the watersplash on its right. The bridge, rebuilt *c*.1938, now covers the whole width of the road. The Longford River flows under the bridge en route to Bushey Park, Hampton Court, where it feeds the Diana Fountain.

120 All Saints' church, Uxbridge Road, opened in 1956. On the left can be seen the roof top of Woodlawn, built for the Pollock family in 1867, becoming the first church in 1935. Woodlawn is now the parish hall to All Saints' church.

121 Miss Nicola Sophia Pollock, photographed *c*.1910. She was the daughter of Mr George Frederick Pollock and lived at Woodlawn, Uxbridge Road until 1915. She died in 1933, aged 78 years and was buried in St George's churchyard.

122 The Girls Friendly Society, which started *c.*1904, photographed in the gardens of Woodlawn, now the site of All Saints' church. Miss Nicola Sophia Pollock was much involved with the Society. She is seated with a black bow at her neck. On her right (next door but one) is Mrs Stannard, headmistress of the Infants School.

123 The Uxbridge Road looking towards Feltham, *c.*1915. The present houses on both sides of the road were not built until the mid- to late 1930s. The wall on the left is part of the Lodge gate into Hanworth Park. This is now the site of the Airparcs recreation centre.

124 Ridge's Stores at 2 Hampton Road, West, *c.*1953, showing shop assistant, Mrs Pearce. The shop is decorated with its Christmas goods. Later known as Clifton Stores, it closed in 1968 and was demolished. Hanworth Library now occupies the site.

125 The Welcome Mission Hall on 4 September 1930, when the new extension was dedicated. The Mission was started by Miss Nicola Sophia Pollock in 1906. It was situated in Hampton Road, West, on the present site of Hanworth library. Miss Pollock owned the Hall until 1925, when she sold it to Mr J. C. Gurr, the Mission's Superintendent. The Mission closed 1962-63.

126 The newly extended Welcome Mission Hall, decorated for Harvest Home in October 1930. A week of Thanksgiving Services was held in the hall which had been decorated by the Young Life Campaigners. The display contained large collections of flowers, fruit and vegetables. One service was taken by Paster Emile Guedj of Paris and the week concluded with the Young Campaigners' conference.

127 Butts Farm, Hampton Road, West, 1895, after its purchase in 1891 by William Whiteley, owner of Whiteley's Store, Bayswater. Together with Glebe Farm, 200 acres provided farms, orchards, market gardens, slaughter houses, canneries, jam making factories and bottling plants. Everything sold in Whiteley's food-hall was produced there [see *The Whiteley Homes Trust*, Phillimore, 1992]. After the murder of William Whiteley, 1907, by his illegitimate son, the site was sold to Mr T.W. Beach, a jam manufacturer. In 1933 New Ideal Homesteads purchased the site for suburban housing.

128 The Butts Farm entrance on Hampton Road, West to Mr Whiteley's fruit farm and factories in 1895. William Whiteley of Whiteley's Store in Queensway purchased Butts and Glebe Farms in 1891, in order to produce everything that was sold in his Queensway store's food-hall.

129 Butts Villas on the Twickenham Road were part of William Whiteley's Hanworth Farms. The cottages survive today. On the side wall of the far cottage the remains of an advert for Whiteley's Store can still be seen.

130   Hampton Road from the boundary with Hampton parish, left of the last house on the left, looking towards the Twickenham Road and the *Hope and Anchor* public house. The terrace of cottages by the lamp post was called Sussex Place. Demolished during the 1960s, the present flats were built by 1971. Today the road is called Hampton Road, East.

131 The Hounslow Road looking towards the bridge over the River Crane, *c*.1910. The river is the boundary between Hanworth and Twickenham. On the far side of the bridge can be seen the roof of the lodge to Hounslow Gunpowder Mills. These functioned *c*.1750-1926. The lodge survives today, as does the shot tower and other remains of the gunpowder mills.

132 The River Crane flowing through the Hounslow Gunpowder Mills in the early years of the last century. Hanworth parish is on the right-hand bank and Twickenham parish is on the left.

BEDFONT

133 Local men outside Minimax on the Staines Road, *c.*1918, waiting for work in the factory. Minimax arrived in Bedfont in 1911, taking over the premises of Elswick Autocar Motor Company. They were bought out by Pyrene Company Ltd. in 1955 and Chubb Fire Security Limited in 1971. The factory was demolished in 1984 and offices and a warehouse now occupy the site.

134 Four workmen, *c.*1900, standing in the doorway of Gibbs' forge, which was on the south side of the Staines Road near the junction with Harlington Road, West. In 1898 Herbert John Gibbs, grandson of the founder, rented the site from Thomas Coles, blacksmith and later purchased it with four adjacent Milestone Cottages. In about 1918, part of the site became a motorcycle agency and repair shop.

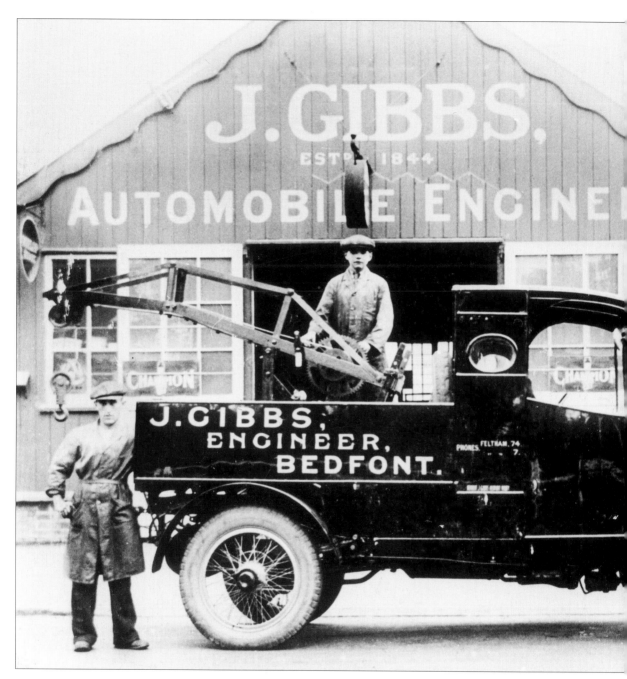

135 John Gibbs came to Bedfont in 1844 as a blacksmith and wheelwright. In the 1920s they became an automobile engineering company and suppliers of agricultural machinery. Situated on the Staines Road, west of the junction with Harlington Road, West, they moved to the Great South West Road by its junction with Stanwell Road after 1925. In September 1997 the firm closed after 153 years.

136 The *Black Dog* public house, Staines Road, west of Gibbs' garage, was there from *c.*1861, replacing an earlier building at the junction of the Staines and Hatton roads. It succeeded the *Dog and Partridge*, which moved *c.*1861 to the Hatton Road. The *Black Dog*, rebuilt 1968, was demolished in 1985 after a fire. Flats now occupy the site.

137 Bedfont police station, *c.*1910, situated on the Staines Road, beside the *Load of Hay* public house. Opened in 1867, it closed in the late 1940s. The building to the right was stabling for the horses. Looking east towards Hounslow, there were no houses on the right.

138 Sub-Divisional Inspector H. Smith, outside Bedfont police station, *c.*1920. This was a sub-divisional station for the Staines, Sunbury and Feltham Division. The Bedfont Police station closed in the 1940s despite protests by local residents. They were assured that a telephone service and transport to Feltham police station would be provided.

139 1, Cherry Orchard Villas, Staines Road, *c.*1914, with possibly Mrs Handscombe and her son in the front garden. From *c.*1914–39 Jessie Handscombe, F.R.H.S., ran a nursery garden and florist's business from the premises. The house survives as 342 Staines Road. The cottage was built between 1865 and 1895.

140 Newhaven, 358 Staines Road, a late 19th-century house, opposite Bedfont Lane, was the home of Nat Gould, *c.*1903-19. A prolific novelist of horse-racing stories, he wrote 150 novels over 30 years. Born in Manchester in 1857, he became a journalist and went to Australia. Returning to England by 1899, he died in July 1919 and was buried in Bradborne, Derbyshire.

141 The Bedfont Baptist Tabernacle, started by the Rev. S. W. Gentle-Cackett in 1896, was completed in 1903. The Rev. Gentle-Cackett is remembered for his work with Armenia after the First World War. He went there on behalf of The Bible Lands Society and brought girls to Bedfont. They lived in bungalows in Bethany Waye and went to Bedfont School.

142 (*Left*) Bedfont War Memorial was unveiled on 11 November 1922 by Major-General Sir George Scott-Moncrieff, Director of Fortifications and Works at the War Office. Built of Portland stone and surmounted by a heraldic lead statue of Victory, it stands 7feet 6inches high. Names of 70 men, who died fighting, are inscribed. It stands in front of the Bedfont Baptist church.

143 (*Right*) Staines Road in the early 1920s, looking east from the turning left into New Road. The War Memorial is seen on the extreme right. The Staines Road did not have a tar-macadamed surface until *c.*1913. The photograph shows that there was no street lighting at that time although the telegraph poles had been there since *c.*1865.

144 (*Below left*) The Parade, Staines Road was built *c.*1900. Bedfont Baptist church is seen in the distance. The shop nearest the church was a newsagent and post office run by Mr William Moore, who first had a shop in New Road. Mr Moore's daughter took over the running of the shop until the late 1960s, when it closed.

145 (*Below right*) The Fairholme estate of almshouses, Staines Road, built *c.*1930s, from a bequest by Elizabeth Jane Jones, widow of Mr Alfred Jones, who ran a pawnbroker's shop in Fulham. Her will left provision for houses for the poor, with no indication of their location. Land was purchased in Bedfont and 72 homes were built. This photograph, *c.*1950, shows the communal hall, provided for social activities.

146 Staines Road looking east from the *Duke's Head* public house, seen right, *c*.1910. The children on the left are on the eastern edge of Bedfont Green. The *Duke's Head* public house was there from the late 18th century to *c*.1930. It was demolished and replaced by the Green garage. This in turn has been replaced by the Murco garage.

147 The Staines Road, looking west, at the start of Bedfont Green on right, *c*.1910. This photograph shows the road before a tar-macadamed surface was laid, *c*.1913. In the distance St Stephen's house can be seen.

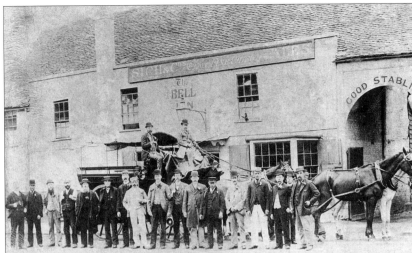

148 The *Bell* inn, Bedfont Green, 1900. The first record of the *Bell* as licensed premises appears in 1724. The Plymouth and Exeter stage coach stopped at the *Bell* to change horses, and passengers would both leave and join the coach. The present public house was built in the early 20th century.

149 The *Bell* inn, *c.*1915, when newly rebuilt. It is now called the *Bell on the Green*.

150 Mr T.H. Powell's grocery and baker's shop, *c.*1920 was situated on the Staines Road, adjacent to the south side of Bedfont Green. Mrs Powell and her daughter are seen in the doorway. The shop opened in the 1890s and the Powell family continued in business into the 1950s.

151 Mr T.H. Powell with his son Baden, standing by his first Ford delivery van, 1918. This had a brass radiator and front solid tyres. It was imported from America and purchased from Crumbles at Staines.

152 View east along the Staines Road, *c.*1905, showing Bedfont Green on left.

153 Buck House, situated near the boundary with Fawns Manor, end-on to the Staines Road, on the south side of the Green, was built as two cottages in the 1830s. William Goymer ran a market garden there from *c.*1900-39. The house was called Charlton Cottage, changing to Buck House, *c.*1909. Mr and Mrs Goymer are seen in the garden, *c.*1920.

154 Ascot coaches passing the Green, en route to the June races. This was a scene repeated every year until 1925, when the Great South West Road opened. By which time the coaches had given way to motor traffic.

155   Looking at Bedfont Green from the turning into Bedfont Road, *c*.1912. The railings on the right form the edge of the Green to the south of the Staines Road. The wall on the left surrounds the garden of St Stephen's.

156   Fawns Manor, a timber-framed building of the mid-16th century, with the 17th-century wing on the right, changed appearance in 1889 with a rendering of Tall's concrete. The manor, first mentioned in 1272, was associated with the Sherborn family from 1437 to 1983, when it was sold to British Airways Housing Association and converted into six flats, with new houses in the grounds.

157 Part of the Edwardian additions to the 18th-century Bedfont House, now called the David Henry Waring Home. The Edwardian additions were built for Mr David Rhiner Waring, who purchased the house in c.1903. After his death in 1930, Miss Roe Waring lived there until her death in 1949. In 1955 it became a local authority residential home.

158 Bennett's Farm, Staines Road is one of the few remaining farmhouses, although its farmlands are now built upon. It was built in 1700 for Richard and John Hatchett; bricks in the ground-floor front wall bear the date, 1700 and the initials R.H. and I.H. Saved from demolition in the early 1970s, when the Hatchett Road houses were built, it was sold and restored.

159 Bedfont Green, *c*.1905, showing the two ponds along the edge of the Staines Road. These were filled-in in the late 1940s. On the left is Bedfont Vicarage, which dated from the 18th century, with Victorian additions. It was replaced by new houses in *c*.1958 and the Vicarage was rebuilt on the adjacent site.

160 Bedfont Fair on the Green, *c.*1900, during Ascot week. It was owned by the Beach family. Until the Great South West Road opened, the route to Ascot from London was via the Staines Road. On their return, the horse-drawn carriages stopped to allow the race-goers to visit the fair. The galloping horse roundabout, seen centre, continued into the late 20th century.

161 Bedfont Green in 1900 with St Mary's church in the centre. This photograph shows the spire before the clock was placed there in 1902 in commemoration of King Edward VII's coronation.

162 The interior of St Mary the Virgin church in the early 20th century, whilst still lit by candles. Gas lighting was installed in 1910 and electricity in 1963. The church is the oldest in the borough of Hounslow, being built c.1150. The chancel arch is original and has Norman chevron decoration.

163 Bedfont Lodge on Bedfont Green, c.1900, was built in 1783 for George Engleheart, Court painter to King George III. His son, Henry, lived in the house after his death. It was the home of Lord Basing in the early 20th century. The house was demolished in 1961 and is now the site of the old peoples' bungalows in Burlington Close.

164 St Stephen's House, situated at the junction of the Hatton Road with the Staines Road, was built *c*.1865 and replaced the *Black Dog* public house, which was rebuilt on the Staines Road, close to the junction with Harlington Road, West. Demolished *c*.1957, it was replaced by modern houses.

165 The garden of St Stephen's House, *c*.1900. It was then the home of the Dove family, seen in the photograph.

166 Pates Manor, in the 1950s, showing the ground-floor Victorian bay windows added in the 1850s. This is the oldest house in the London Borough of Hounslow, with the wing on the right being a medieval hall house of pre–1500. The wing at right angles was built in *c*.1550. The house was purchased and restored by the late Mr Francis Clive-Ross in 1964.

167 Part of the garden of Pates Manor in 1955. The cedar tree survives but the low knot hedge garden in the foreground disappeared in the 1960s.

168 One of the farm barns at Pates Manor. There was a farm attached to the manor house, but in the 1920s much of the farm lands were sold for building development. The barn was demolished in the early 1960s for the building of the houses in Longleat Way, completed in 1963.

169 The Spinney, Stanwell Road, was two early 19th-century cottages converted into one dwelling for the Gibbs family. Mr Reginald Gibbs and his family lived there from *c*.1950. Reginald is seen in the centre with his brothers Murray on the left and Sidney on the right. In the 1980s, after Mr and Mrs Gibbs died, the house was demolished.

170 Herbert John Gibbs, grandson of John Gibbs, who started the blacksmith's business in 1844 on the Staines Road. Herbert ran the Gibbs' business until the mid-1930s. He lived in the Spinney until his death in 1938.

171 New Road in the 1920s looking south from the junction with the Hatton Road. New Road was built linking the Staines Road with Hatton Road in the 1870s.

172 Mr Harry Ford standing outside his family's butcher shop at 85 New Road, by the turning into Page Road. The shop opened in the 1880s and was run by the Ford family until it closed in 1988.

173 49 New Road is a semi-detached house, part of Monzie Villas, built in 1882. This photograph shows female members of the family living there in the early 1900s.

174 The Two Bridges in the Hatton Road in 1929, looking towards the turning into New Road on the left. The bridge on the right has the Duke of Northumberland's River flowing underneath. The bridge on the left is over the Longford River. Both rivers are man-made.

175 One of the Two Bridges, Hatton Road, 1932, showing the watersplash in the Duke of Northumberland's River, used as a paddling pool by local children. The brickwork on the right is the edge of the bridge over the Longford River. The bridges are shown on John Rocque's Map of Middlesex of 1754. They were replaced by one bridge in 1971.

176 The thatched cottage, Hatton Road by the two bridges, photographed in the 1950s. This cottage was the only thatched house left in Bedfont. It was replaced by the Two Bridges Hostel in the early 1970s. It is shown on the 1839 Tithe map for Bedfont as two cottages.

177 Bedfont National School in the Hatton Road opened in 1847. It was built on land given by Colonel William Reed of Burlington House on Bedfont Green. On the extreme left was the Headmaster's House and on the right, the infant and girls' classroom. This building was in use until the present school was built on an adjacent site in 1951.

178 The Bedfont National School staff in 1900. Mr Robert Pickering, the Headmaster, is seen centre, back row, with Mrs Pickering on his left. He was Headmaster 1886-1926. The staff in the back row from the left are: Mr Merrick, Miss Penn, Miss Brangwyn. Front row from the left: Miss Davis, Miss Hackney. Miss N. Dunkley and Miss C. Penn. Seated, left, is Miss Dunkley.

179 Cain's Lane from the Great South West Road looking south to the Hatton Road, running across the top of photograph in *c.*1938, showing semi-detached houses being built by R. T. Warren. These sold at £495. Cain's Lane ran north across the present London (Heathrow) Airport, to the Bath Road by the *Magpies* public house.

HATTON

180 Hatton Road by the turning for Cain's Lane in 1949 showing the first B.O.A.C. Boeing 377 Stratocruiser coming in to land at Heathrow. Stratocruisers were then the largest civil airliners in the world and the only double-decked ones. B.O.A.C. used them on their London–New York route from December 1949.

181 The first Hatton Baptist Church, *c.*1900, situated on the Hatton Road, close to the *Wellington* inn. It was built *c.*1880 and was replaced by the present church *c.*1934.

182 Hatton Band of Hope, formed in 1880, photographed in June 1912, attending the South West Middlesex Band of Hope Union Summer Fête and Sports. This was held in the Riding School grounds at Whitton Dene.

183 The *Green Man* at Hatton in the 1930s. Parts of this building dated back to the 17th century, when it had a thatched roof. At present the public house is undergoing alterations.

184 Mr Otto Dietrich and his son, William, outside their cottage in Faggs Road, Hatton, *c.*1928. Mr Dietrich made, maintained and raced penny-farthing bicycles. He was a familiar figure cycling on his penny-farthing around Bedfont and Hatton, where he provided a home service of shaving and hair-cutting.

185 St Anthony's Home, a Roman Catholic orphanage at Hatton, *c*.1920. Originally a 19th-century cottage, it was purchased in 1834 by Sir Frederick Pollock who extended it as his family increased, naming it Temple Hatton in 1869. His widow died there in 1895 and it was sold to become the orphanage. This closed and the site was sold in 1958, being demolished in *c*.1960.

186 The River Crane watersplash in Dockwell Lane, Hatton, *c*.1910. This disappeared in 1925 when the Great South West Road opened. A bridge now takes the River Crane underneath the road.

187 Hatton Cross, the Great South West Road in the 1950s, showing the garage demolished for the building of Hatton Cross underground station, on the Piccadilly line extension from Hounslow West to Heathrow Airport, completed in 1975.

188 The Great South West Road opened in 1925, taking traffic from the newly opened Great West Road westwards to the town of Staines. This general view of the Great South West Road, *c.*1950, shows it prior to widening into a dual carriageway, *c.*1955.

189 The Zuyder Zee roadhouse, Great South West Road, *c.*1950, prior to demolition in *c.*1954 for widening of the road into a dual carriageway. The bungalow, right of the windmill, was the first building completed after the opening of the road in 1925. Called the Floral tearooms in 1929, it became the Zuyder Zee in *c.*1936, with dancing nightly from 8.30p.m.

190 The *Dog and Partridge* public house in the 1920s.. This was situated on the west side of the Hatton Road, close to the boundary with Harlington parish. The public house was built *c.*1860 and was demolished for the building of Heathrow Airport in 1945.

Index

Roman numerals refer to pages in the introduction, arabic numerals to individual illustrations.

STREET PLAN OF
FELTHAM

Scale of ½ Mile

¼   ½

Urban District Boundary ·—·—·—·